Awakenings
Volume 1

By Brian Bucks

Copyright © 2016 Brian Bucks

All rights reserved.

With this statement included the material may be copied for personal use:
"This material may be copied without charge for non-commercial, non-resale personal use only. For all other uses contact the author or publisher Bucks Enterprises – Services and Training, INC., 90444 CR H, Mitchell, NE. All rights reserved, copyrighted material © 2016."

Bucks Enterprises – Services and Training, INC.
90444 County Road H
Mitchell, NE. 69357

ISBN: 0692705953
ISBN-13: 978-0692705957

Printed in the U.S.A.
First Printing – July 2016

Cover photograph © 2016 Brian Bucks
Image of Waterfall at Yellowstone National Park.

To Colleen, my wife, for the beauty of her courage and fierce love.

To our children – Alison, Ezekiel, and Abigail – that they find courage earlier than I have to express their own "voice," risk exploring, and act on it.

CONTENTS

PREFACE	IX
PURITY	1
GRADUATION DAYS	2
CURB APPEAL	3
RUTS	3
NOT JUST	4
WHAT IF?	4
MILESTONES	5
JARRING OF JOURNEY	5
FLOATING	6
HIGHWAY 26	6
PUSHING PEBBLES	6
FULL FACED	7
GRAY LIGHT OF DAWN	7
BUZZWORD BINGO	8
END OF DAY	8
NAVIGATE	9
SPRING SNOW	10
THE STARE	11
STEW	12
EVOKING	13
DEPENDENCY	14
GIVE AND TAKE	15
ETERNITY TO ETERNITY	15
TIME AGAIN	16
GIFT OF DAY	16
GRATITUDE	16
GUSTS	17

GREAT POETS	17
TECHNOLOGY	18
BEAR	18
RUSTED	18
HAPPY	19
TRICKLE	19
BARRIERS	19
BROKEN PEOPLE	20
MAKE ROOM	20
EARLY SPRING	20
PRESENT	21
BLAME AND SUFFERING	22
BLAME	22
VOICE	23
POWER OF VOICE	23
BONDS	24
LIGHT ABSORBED	24
SIMPLE AND COMPLEX	25
ENGLISH LIT	25
WITHIN THE WALLS	26
THE PLACE THAT ROARS	26
THE GRASS WEEPS	27
FROST ON THE CAR	27
SICK	28
BUBBLES	28
MARCH SNOW	29
OATMEAL RAISIN COOKIES	29
GRAY	30
RECKONING	30
BETROTHED	31

BODY PACES	31
WRESTLING	32
ALIVE	33
BROWN LEAVES	34
GRIT	34
BLUE TENT	35
SHARDS	36
MOON JELL-O	37
EARLY MORNING	38
BEAUTY ALL AROUND	38
FLOCK	39
INVISIBLE MAN	40
COME TO HIM	40
FLAMING TURKEY OR ODE TO DIFFERENTIAL RELAYS	41
HEART BROKER	42
COYOTES	42
FAITH IS	43
HIGHWAY 85 NORTH OF CHEYENNE	43
FORTITUDE	44
PIVOT	45
EBBINGS	46
WHAT DOES HEART SAY	47
QUID PRO QUO	48
LEGACY	49
OLD RED TRACTOR	50
DAILY GRIND	50
ANXIETY	51
FIRE IN THE HOLE	51
MUD	52
SOFT SKY	52

BEHOLDING	53
PRAY	53
WEIGHT AND WAIT	54
TRANSPARENCY	54
COYOTE CARCASS	55
DANCED	55
MATURITY	56
LOOSE CANNON	57
DREAMS	58
LETTING GO	58
SOMETHING NEW	59
ENDURANCE	60
DOG DAYS	61
SMALL THINGS	62
ICE	62
COLD WIND	63
SUNDAY MORNING	63
28 YEARS	64
SPACE BETWEEN DESIRES AND EXPECTATIONS	65
CRACK THE SHELL – CORE EXPOSED	66
MOLLY - 1/2 BORDER COLLIE AND 1/2 PYRENEES	67
SILENCE	67
BROKEN WORDS - ONE FOR ALL AND ALL FOR ONE	68
VEILED	69
FRAGILE	69
RAW	70
ABOUT THE AUTHOR	73

PREFACE

One of the things on my bucket list had been to create a blog. It marked the ending of one season and the beginning of a new one. This project is mostly a compilation of poems from my daily blog.

I look forward to sharing these poems and the exploration it brings. My personal focus is on "awakenings" and "intentionality" for 2016. So here is to exploration and small beginnings.

Before I get to the poems, as I reflect back on the past year I wanted to share a couple of resources that left an imprint on me.

The first is a book by David Schnarch called *Passionate Marriage: Keeping Love and Intimacy Alive in Committed Relationships.* This book has been quite enlightening; isn't a quick read; and isn't for the faint of heart or those who are easily offended. The truths in it can lead to transformation.

The second is a podcast by The Allender Center from February 28, 2015 titled *Naming and Reflecting the Beauty of God in Our Stories.* I have listened to this multiple times, it just puts things in perspective. Resources from The Allender Center have proven to be effective in processing healing for me through trauma, telling of my own story, and restoration of my soul.

The third is Ransomed Heart Boot Camp. I attended one last year and found it to be quite valuable.

Brian Bucks
May 2016
Western Nebraska

Purity

snow falls
white velcro
sticky clean
purity's stickiness

landing on all
everyone, everything belongs
adorned in innocence
wedding day white

spring's blossoms didn't ask
yet cleanly coated
beauty to gaze upon
eyes drawn to heavy limbs
weighed with purity

walk among the sacred
allow self to be glazed
purity invites participation
engage in the joy and anticipation

Graduation Days

Occasionally with cap and gown.
Most often just invisible crown.
Life is an education we all know.
Wrestling moments seem terribly slow.

Season's transition.
Requires different position.
Endings happen sooner than think.
At new beginnings brink.

Some graduations accompanied with a diploma.
All accompanied by struggle.
The first breath and last breath.
Cycle of life and death.

Shedding of skin.
Shifting residence of eternity with grimace or grin.
Intentional and awake is our choice.
Steward your life and voice.

Curb Appeal

Curb Appeal
Is what I see real?

Dressed up exterior.
Fascia covers crumbling interior.

Infrastructure waits repair.
So many years of lack of care.

Buyer beware.
Open house exposes what's bare.

Fascia of soul.
Hiding holes.

Internal repair.
Work of self-care.

Ruts

Sometimes ruts provide the only way forward.
Sometimes trailblazing and leaving ruts.
Sometimes praying please don't let me be first.
Sometimes path is treacherous when first.
Sometimes ruts are the only thing keeping me on the road.
Can't follow ruts blindly or may end up in ditch.
Slogging through mud and standing water.
Ruts give courage to keep going, if stop stuck.
Stuck in rut when stop, no traction - lots of motion, no movement.
When weather is fair curse the ruts, makes journey rough.
When weather is foul embrace the ruts, makes journey viable.

Not Just

All that envelops.
Crispy and burn.
Sunburned skin peels.
New garment adorns.
Clean, fresh, born again.
Not just a moment.
New way of life.
Each day begin anew.
Simple and complex.
Paradox of spirit, soul, mind, and heart.

What If?

Discovering power.
Recreate memory.
Different outcome.

What if?

What if?
Love expressed
      instead of abuse?

What if?
Imagination plays
      recreates what could be?

What if?
Truth exchanged
      for lies.

What if?
God's interpretation
      a peripety for mine?

Milestones

A milestone reached today.
25 years of service belayed.
Career never foreseen.
Journey wildly careened.
Rare to work one place.
Stress weathered face.
Regrets exchanged for peace.
Gratitude lubricates life with grease.
Rural place a family grew.
Past season fades as dew.
All launching out to explore.
Adventures await on new shores.

Jarring of Journey

Jarring of journey awakens from slumber.
A matter of time before life has your number.
Hitting the wall in similar ways.
Breaks down pride, now so frayed.
Rattled and shaken.
There is no mistaken.
Suffering plays a part.
Restarting the heart.
Avoid the truth averting pain.
Wasting your story and all that can gain.
Agreeing with Truth, a way to start.
Courage to leave old, depart.
Mental gyrations as struggle and strive.
Sorrow and grief boil alive.
Dividing dross from gold.
Chapters in your story yet to be told.

Floating

As bounce up and down the field hawk nearby.
Hovers above hunting, so still could be a kite.
As he watches from the old bales we eye each other.
Each trip down the field he stays a little longer.
Stays until close enough to use phone to catch pictures.
Finally I get to close and takes flight.
As return back down the field there he sits again.
I disturb mice and gophers, opportunities for a snack.
Simple things remind of earthiness of life.

Highway 26

Turkeys everywhere today.
Darting out on the road.
Tom's strutting in full display.
Eyes roam as drive.
Creation pulls vision.
River valley full of life.

Pushing Pebbles

Memories surge pushing each pebble.
Polished and smooth in wash of life.
Past, present, future caught in current of time.
Sharp edges of past worn.
No cut to "it" anymore.
Congruence of beginning, middle, end.
Past resides in the past.
Previous chapter of story complete.
Consequences impact the present.
New beginnings are possible today.
Story's plot changes radically starting today.

Full Faced

Moon rises full faced.
Crests the hill, sun wanes.
Sounds of dusk.
Pheasants call, owl hoots.
Pack of coyotes yelping in glee.
A type of peace radiates from creation.
His presence is evident.
Warmth of favorite sweatshirt.
Surrounds, envelops in peace.
Finally the resting place after four and a half years.
Grueling journey with sweetness at pause.
Not the same person started as.
Started as two dimensional cutout.
Now three dimensional - alive.

Gray Light of Dawn

Fog and frost paint the air.
Filtered gray light of dawn.
Yields to brilliant sun.

Another morning to empty cares.
By nature's beauty drawn.
Another day's race to run.

Discover new depth of relationship share.
Live in the moment before it's gone.
Live in awe, allow it to stun.

Buzzword Bingo

What once enjoyed as a profession,
Lost interest, no longer interested in the confession.
Removed from work by bureaucratic minutia,
Hours spent bleeding ink color of fuchsia.
So many hands in the pie,
Not even a scrap for mice, just left to die.
Resources drained before actual work starts,
All the hubbub without any heart.
Buzzword bingo fills the air,
Sounds really good, nobody cares.
Can smile at the use of lingo,
Exposes not as smart as a dingo.

End of Day

End of the day and wind must howl,
One's spirit grows foul.
All of the wind tests one's nerve,
Easy to distract, redirect and swerve.

Push of gust makes one huff,
Become agitated and gruff.
Such a beautiful morning at the start,
Each hour that passes mind pricked with dart.

Wind in the ear,
Draws up boiling fear.
Constant gnawing of the bone,
Exposing heart of stone.

Face the wind,
Allow its bend.
Tumbleweeds of soul,
Blown away, uprooted path to whole.

Navigate

Navigate the terrain,
Singing a new refrain.
New imprint on the brain,
Healthy now, no longer profane.

Utterly awakened,
No mistake'n.
An endurance race,
New pace to embrace.

New skills and tools,
True North of soul precious jewel.
Confound the keepers of secrets,
Freedoms torrents, wept.

Lost no more,
Landmarks galore.
Explore familiar venues,
Satisfying new menus.

Spring Snow

Snow falls heavily from sky,
Thick and wet drifting down.
Leaving trees and blossoms coated,
White frosting with coconut sprinkled on it.
Fluffy looking, pure whiteness,
Devoid of violation.
Left in awe of beauty as intended,
Unspoiled and holy to the eye.

Later I will go walk Molly,
We will tromp through the snow.
She will be a puppy again,
Renewed by fresh purity.

I will watch and be present,
Pure covering changes context.
Birds will sound different,
Green of alfalfa and grass,
Accentuated by several inches of snow.

Horses huddled together,
Damp as snow melts against their shedding winter coats.
Perhaps little drifts collecting on the ridge of their backs.

Be present, moment won't last.
In a day all will be melted.
Just a faint memory left.
Beauty remembered as life expressed.

Words just spill out easy this morning,
Taken with creation's ecstasy.
Passion awoke in young feeling.
All created by early Spring snow.
Friskiness of being alive,
Memories of seasons past.
Snow draws them to mind just as a song or smell.
Draws the past into the present.

Integrating the moments together,
Bringing a sense of wholeness.

The Stare

With my eyes I can change the momentum.
Crouching I redirect the herd with a stare.
Intensity personified thriving in job created for.
Playful passion expressed.
Always feel young.
Fierce wildness of loyalty.
Attunement to relationship of pack and herd.
Affirmation of a soft rub around neck.
Eyes pierce into being, man-canine connection.
Senses the joy in expression of face.
Brings frisbee to draw me into young playful place.
Present in the moment, experiencing life.
I am the Border Collie.

Stew

Internal places brew,
Tenderized meaty stew.
Heat turned up,
Seasoning interrupts.

Stir and taste,
Simmers into spicy paste.
Crispness fails with time,
Flavor leaks out as slime.

Soul tested in the flame,
Learn to drop the shame.
Allow the marination,
Embrace the consternation.

Evoking

All that is buried,
'Cause no longer can carry.
Deeper into soul dig each spade of dirt,
Mistakenly believe can bury the hurt.

Reaching up from that grave,
Longings and desires crawl out of that cave.
What's been buried isn't dead,
Hibernating in thoughts deep in head.

Voice slowly returns,
Anger at self-spurned.
Fury and rage crescendo,
Soul reluctantly opens window.

Evoking a frown,
Burdens laid down.
Lazarus of soul called from tomb,
Grave clothes wrapped tightly, a womb.

Can't believe how long persisted,
Debris of life resisted.
Out of darkness new life,
Peace replaces internal strife.

His voice calls forth,
That which was dead to live again.
Unburied each shovel of dirt,
Painful healing of places been hurt.

Joy evoked,
Where once it was choked.
Hope again,
Reconciliation with who I've been.

Dependency

What am I dependent on?
Who am do I look to?
Why do I choose those people or things?
If I'm honest how much is idolatrous?

Filling an empty place.
Not leaving room for God's grace.
My gaze fixed on another.
Missing all He longs to uncover.

What do I gain by filling that space,
With all that numbs instead of His embrace?
Freedom in acknowledging truth,
Worship given to "idols."

That is a start,
Of uncovering my heart.
Discovering what can be,
Live in the present and freshly see.

Give and Take

I give you take,
Not balanced just fake.
One sided relationships break,
Robs soul, being leaks.
Made for community,
Narcissism feeds disunity.
Searching for like-minded ones,
New relationships begun.
Mutual give and take,
From this healthy make.

Eternity to Eternity

From eternity to eternity,
With a stop at humanity.
Remember from where we came,
One day we return re-framed.
The good, the bad, and the ugly,
Woven together in beauty.
Each strand by itself isn't whole,
So much story knitted in soul.
Integrated into the present,
Let go of interpretation and resentment.
The future and all yet to be,
Past, present, future formed into one from three.
Redemption, restoration, reconciliation,
Bind together in eternity's present station.

Time Again

It's time again,
Spring spurts sublime.
From bud to blossom,
Resurrection so awesome.
In matter of days,
Dormant now alive and gay.
Being filled with redolence,
No longer Winter's snow fence.
Wild plums burst with life,
White purity of petals rife.

Gift of Day

Gift of day,
Brisk air opens to play.
See herd of deer,
Senses become clear.
Eyes open to what fear,
Open ears to what hear.

Gratitude

Many things to be grateful for,
As explore find so much more.
Gift of life to live,
No longer bound so much to give.
Imagination pushes doors,
Opening up hidden stores.
Stronger than ever knew,
Giants melted just left a dew.

Gusts

Invisible gusts push van around,
Sways and rocks losing attachment to ground.
Dirt paints invisible,
Makes day miserable.
Western Nebraska's radical temperature shifts,
Carves out landscapes - explore the gifts.
Barren vistas funnel the wind,
Blowing past far behind.

Great Poets

Find myself in the library.
Across from great poets.
Contained in the books.
Though long dead words still live.
Reminding me voice has eternal element.
In university far from home.
Western edge of South Dakota voices still speak.
Thoreau and Angelou stare at me from the shelf.
Coincidence I sit at the table and look up?
Having to pick the book off the shelf.
Feel the paper and see their voice.
Beckoning for the thirsty to drink.
Awakens the sleepy soul.

Technology

Engineering, nerding out.
Complicated control systems touted.
Reality of reliability and security compromised.
Technology doesn't always improve our lives.
Decision makers sold snake oil.
Promises that make knowledgeable recoil.
Doing more with less is fallacy.
Drank the Kool-Aid™ self-inflicted malady.

Bear

A faithful friend over the years,
Always greets me, bringing cheer.
Many seasons have sped by,
He's slowed down yet not shy.
To see him basking in the sun,
Warmth of Spring limberly runs.
Many memories come to mind,
Just an echo faintly find.

Rusted

Internal course change,
Integration everything rearranged.
Happiness found,
New peace abounds.
Interior logjam busted,
Oil loosens all that's rusted.

Happy

An internal job,
External seeking robs.
Places once numb,
Treated self as bum.
Pain as awaken and come alive,
What once was dead now thrives.
Happiness wells up inside,
Free of shame and need to hide.
Energy of secrets liberated,
Chain reaction created.
Awakened places of coma of soul,
Journey challenging, emptying yet full.
Meshing together places that grind,
Joy in integration of body, soul, and mind.

Trickle

Sound of water.
Just a trickle.
Snow melts into gutter.
Sounds refreshing.
Spring is here.

Barriers

Each day a new barrier to get work done,
One more person demanding a change, work no longer fun.
Bureaucrats who don't want confused with facts,
Becomes a power trip for all their hacks.
Process not vetted by end-users so broken at the start,
See life force of workers sink and lose heart.

Broken People

Broken people everywhere,
Burdens heavy full of care.
Redemption comes into this space,
Light in darkness fear's displaced.
When hope wavers,
Remember your Savior.
Three days in,
New life begins.

Make Room

Empty tomb,
Make Him room.
Burden carried in between,
Lay it at His feet, come clean.

Early Spring

Easter comes early this year,
Tomorrow celebrate resurrection, the cost so dear.
Snow covers the ground today,
Between crucifixion and resurrection place of gray.
Moment when all seems lost,
Lay burdens at foot of cross.
Tomorrow the tombstone is rolled away,
Bringing hope to all gone astray.
Whiteness of snow,
A cleansing we can know.
Beauty exchanged for our sorrow,
Joy in living today and tomorrow.

Present

Storm of emotion and rage,
Passes quickly, difficult to gauge.
Where did that come from trapped within?
Let it pass, pain released no longer singe.
Stay present, rage is from past.
Can hold it, explore it as if three dimensional construct.
Wow look at that place, how odd.
Surreal to detach and not be swept away with it.
No longer mine to carry, burden free of.
Live in a place of surrender, touch the pain trapped in present.
Yet don't have to live in the past.
No more catatonic state dwelling in past.
Been rescued and redeemed from that place.
Live in present grace and mercy.
Do what it takes to stay present.
Release ambivalence, no longer scapegoat.
No longer keeper of family secrets.
No longer held in catatonic place.
Present, alive, survived.
Story redeemed, set free.
In the present there is joy.
In the present there is hope.
In the present there is love.
In the present safe.

Blame and Suffering

A twisting of blame hamstrings being able to live, to be alive. A weight and burden that no longer need to carry. It is Good Friday, the day we celebrate Jesus bearing the weight of our suffering, pain, sin, being scapegoated, being victimized. Isaiah 53:3 (KJV) – "He is despised and rejected of men, a man of sorrow, and acquainted with grief: and we hid as it were our faces from him; he was despised and we esteemed him not."

Jesus is familiar with our suffering, he experienced it all on our behalf so we would never be alone or forsaken. Bring your burdens to the foot of the cross today and place it at his feet, for him to judge and interpret; no longer needing to pick it up and carry it anymore. BE FREE from it TODAY.

Blame

When attribute someone's over reaction or lack of control,
To who I am or what I've done – BLAME – reality stole.
A black eye of blame,
In enters shame.
Carry a burden not mine,
Blind to hook, wallow as swine.
Pulled back to the past,
Happens so incredibly fast.
Hook so deep and pain is numb,
Such an internal scrum.
Freeing the barb,
Excruciatingly hard.
Set will to be free finally start,
Awakening, pain of frostbite in heart.
Intentional and resolute,
Courage and voice no longer mute.

Voice

Voice goes off line,
Instantly before logic can say it's fine.
Triggered a memory trapped in soul,
Feel it in body still living unwhole.
Can't express what is happening,
Held hostage to brain and body reacting.
Exhaustion and stress carried in core,
No longer needed yet can't just ignore.
Haunts and hounds at "random" spark,
Pent up energy leaving its mark.
Realizing it isn't anxiety feel,
Bound up pain that needs healed.
Pay attention to body it speaks,
Where memory fails pain peaks.

Power of Voice

Power of voice.
Reveal story, no other choice.
Deny story, fragment apart.
Own story, healing starts.
Ugliness of own history.
Give it your voice.
Get lost in places hid.
Tell the whole, not just some.
Rest in TRUTH, feel breath and sigh.
Voice out of mercy and love.
No longer carry burden of story.
Congruent integration unfolds from story told.
Comes from authentic inner place.
Silence broken, words honor with grace.

Bonds

Broken bonds of life,
Twisted and contorted strife.
Truth of story lost,
Pay a personal cost.
Tell the story,
Even the gory.
False interpretations exposed,
True story composed.
Reality has a way of breaking lies,
Freedom's shout and cry.
Silenced voice no more,
Loosed at internal core.

Light Absorbed

Softness of morning air,
Gentle light absorbed.
Walking gingerly with no cares,
Creation meant to be adored.
Centered in calm,
Often find peace in storm.
Surrender and give alms,
In my daybreak norm.

Simple and Complex

Beauty of the simple.
Elegance of complex.
Beauty and elegance woven together.
Complements and strengthen what could stand alone.
Stronger together.
Congruent and integrated.
Powerful integrity without words.
Draws others, an open invitation.
Sweetness of safe community.
Fortitude to risk vulnerability, being known.
Smoothing roughness of character.
Soothing to soul, redemption.
Sought after and invited.
Peace settles from inside out.

English Lit

Ides of March draws me back to high school,
Where our teacher drew us into the world of Shakespeare.
Decades later still have fond memories,
A love for different types of literature discovered.

Our high school lit class just as difficult as college class,
Teacher's love of literature wouldn't allow less.
Discussions and discovery as new worlds opened,
Exploration of Human Nature and motive awakened.

Within the Walls

Why does "it" stay within the walls,
If it's legit then take it out in halls.
In the highways and byways,
To the thirsty and hungry, humanity's strays.

All the gifts feeding the full,
Become so numb and dull.
Doesn't appeal anymore,
Narcissistic and empty need restored.

Lost in all the good gifts,
Focus to sift and re-shift.
Loss of first love,
Need renewed from above.

The Place That Roars

How pull back in moment where roar,
Back down and hesitate return to safe shores.
Interpret roar as not enough and blame,
When truth is another person's younger self emoting pain.

What if roar isn't about me?
What if roar is about getting free?
Defiance expressed is about places trapped,
All the baggage needs unpacked.

I am safe no matter the roar,
In the moment we both are restored.
Reactions change as mature,
Both are grounded and secure.

The Grass Weeps

Grass on ditch bank kneeling prayerfully.
Rain and snow forced it down.
Weary and weeping, bowed at the edge.
Damp, recent heaviness.

Sun is out and tall tufts over a foot long glisten.
Moistness of contrasting dirt with brown blades.
Accentuated in softness of breaking dawn.
Spring soon will come and burden just a memory.

Frost on the Car

Frost on the car, unique scar.
Finger of divine etched the design.
Feathery fern impressed by the unknown.
Few more moments and would be puddles.

Erased clean as if never seen.
A gift of beauty to refocus the day.
Always something to re-center, challenge the heart.
Show up in the moment prepare for the day.

Sick

Tired of being sick, looking out window.
Only so much introspection into portal of soul.
Mental rest, physical rest, emotional rest, spiritual rest.
Caring for the soul, entire being.

Confronted with all ways comfort when sick.
Yet not all ways of comfort restore the soul.
Looking outside and wishing could be there.
Wide open space soul can explore.

Places of beauty and joy resuscitates spirit.
Warmth of sun nurturing all that lives.
Feeling its hot rays cultivates gratitude.
A soft, warm breath soaks into depths of soul.

Bubbles

Memories bubble to surface,
Life giving springs rising.
Invitation to draw a drink,
Revisit the past and integrate.

Stepping into the memory,
New perspectives to explore.
Investigate old surroundings,
Surreal instant in time no more.

Harm held in memory,
Released in the Truth.
Trauma loses power,
Soul more whole.

March Snow

Familiar sense when walk out the door to a March snow,
Drawn back in time to teenager.
Something about the look, smell, and beauty of youth,
Pulls a youngness to the surface.

Contrasts all around,
Green of grass pierces snow.
Disked fields, chocolate cake with thin vanilla frosting,
Snow melts rapidly.

Gray sky soon to give way,
Anticipation of sun bursting through.
Doves perched together cooing,
Horses neighing, acknowledging me.

Quietness of non-mechanical,
Only sounds are of living things.
Trees resisting the wind,
Footsteps on gravel.

Oatmeal Raisin Cookies

Simpler times recall,
Grandma making cookies.
Our hands helping put dough on cookie sheets,
Oatmeal raisin and peanut butter cookies.
Ruined for any other cookies, they just aren't grandma's.
Memories fade with time, yet some are triggered,
With the smell of cookies baking, or others close to their texture.
A smile to the face, something time can never take.

Gray

Warmth of late morning gives way,
Distant horizon fades to gray.
Season confused if Winter or Spring,
Ambivalence that nature brings.

Can see the approaching transition,
Animals sense, they feed before reposition.
Wind driven rain pelts windows,
Temperature drops begging snow.

Reckoning

When the past comes knocking,
When past and present collide.
Confronted with who once was,
Reckon with who now am.

Reckoning determines future journey,
If resist and deny what's been and what is – worlds collide.
Incongruence and stress work damage on soul,
Turmoil until release and let go.

Peace comes in the place that past is the past,
Today let it go, no longer defines.
Yes it was, but no longer has power,
Truthful and honest past lost its control.

Untwisted and unraveled to be who I am,
No longer in bondage to all that's been.
Free to explore and go to new places,
Internally light after such a long night.

Betrothed

To believe worth committing to,
A crucible of two.
Space created of fiery love,
Mingle and mix with heaven above.

Valued and pursued,
Free to be, no longer used.
Honored and validated,
Union together celebrated.

Body Paces

Eyes heavy and dry,
Can't sleep even though try.
Mind races,
Body paces.

Cycle goes around,
Explore but nothing found.
No escape from past,
Flooded by regret so fast.

Big picture twisted and bent,
Stuck on replay of event.
Rational thought yields,
Interpretation in left field.

Wrestling

Wrestle in that place of incongruence,
Between good and evil and what "it" means.
My heart is good,
Yet action don't always match.

The warring of what that "means,"
About who I am.
Black and white thinking,
All good or all bad.

Interpretations and where I take them,
Choices about cycles that find self in.
Not about stopping or controlling cycles,
It's about which cycle.

Moment where choose healthy,
Moment where choose unhealthy.
Neither defines who I am or my heart,
Just expression of inner struggle.

How did it get so convoluted?
Attaching value and worth to actions and performance.
Instead of attaching value and worth of who I am with self, God, and others.
That inner place where get stuck playing the event over and over.

The *Ground Hog Day* moments relived over and over.
Replay it until reconciled in being.
It doesn't define my heart.

I am more than a performance or action.
I am human, a person, a man.
I sin, fail, make wrong choices.
I am good, do right, succeed, and make right choices.

I am not defined by either sin or good.
My heart is good and right with God.

I am an expression of who I Am created me to be.
Loving, caring, passionate, strong, weak, dependent, independent, attached, and connected.

Alive

Gift of alive, sun on my face,
In spite of myself receive undeserved grace.
Reminded of awe as meadowlark sings,
Simplicity of its praises melodically rings.

Pastoral surroundings, horses lazily graze,
In gift of warmth on late Winter's day.
Hush falls at times and draws my ears,
Then crescendo of creation's rustle becomes clear.

So much to be grateful for,
So much life yet to explore.
Love yet to discover,
All to be known and uncovered.

This day will never be again,
Gratefulness wears a smile and grins.
No matter what comes today,
Find that place of gratitude to display.

Brown Leaves

Brown frayed leaves angrily dance,
Driven by whipping gusts.
Made to perform and dance,
Fulfilling another's desires and lusts.

Winter's grip fades,
Leaves uncovered in thaw.
All that snow shades,
Branches of ground discovered raw.

Green of grass exposed,
Memory gradually heals.
Slowly leaves decompose,
Scarred, wound no longer feel.

Winter will give way,
New life of Spring so clean.
Seasons change in a day,
Compost of fall redeemed.

Grit

Dirt in eyes,
Wonder why?
Grit of life,
Internal strife.

Clear cries,
Words fly.
Mental rut,
Emotionally cut.

Blue Tent

The blue tent against barren trees,
White stones dot the hill in the soft breeze.
Hearse will come soon,
Plant the shell in the tomb.

Quietness in moments wait,
Processions come and go for this date.
Always ends the same,
Casket our body reclaims.

Dirt tossed with hollow echo,
Each a gentle blow.
Soft dirt on a Winter's day,
Piled freshly on a grave.

Shards

Introspection is not protection,
Life doesn't come with directions.
Navigating life without a safety net,
Risk and courage or just fret.

Push the boundary of what has been,
Explore new places and dive right in.
One big jump and plunge in deep,
All resistance begins to seep.

Life to live and love to grow,
Humble self, make self low.
Pride prevents being known,
Projects a garish clown.

Exposure softens all that's hard,
Heart revealed, all its broken shards.
Put back together in new way,
Be thankful for another breath today.

Moon Jell-O

Moon rests like a banana slice,
Above a Jell-O™ bed of blue and pink.
Crystal clear stillness beauty of great price,
Once again gratitude and grace beyond the brink.

Today is the moment to live,
All that's been withheld to give.
Overcome fear to dwell in mourning,
New robes to wear and adorning.

Caught by beauty in the light,
Takes away to new heights.
Soul awakens from the blight,
Finds salvation and delight.

Early Morning

Moon bright through translucent clouds,
Early morning lit by fullness so proud.
Lesser light hovers low,
Begrudgingly, going slow.

Perfect early morning for a walk,
Wish my love would come and talk.
To steal a moment before the day,
Time for us to share hopes and pray.

Gift of a day to embrace,
Nice to share face to face.
Coolness of air upon our skin,
Reminds us each day a gift again.

Beauty All Around

Evening light, sun low in sky,
Rainbow cloud catches my eye.
Geese flying into sun,
Swallowed up, blurred into one.

Gift of today in beauty all around,
Open up soul, allow self to be found.
Captured in an instant full of awe,
Creation's bounty fresh and raw.

Awakens what's so easily lost,
Just slow down and see is all it costs.
Peace enters in quiet and quick,
Jars busy brain with a subtle kick.

Flock

Laugh at border collie laying on cusp of ditch,
Body contracted tight, spring like.
Sheep in field at edge, near road,
Shepherd stands as a statue.
Dog close by being itself.
Dog's oneness with shepherd and sheep.
Symbiotic beauty observed.
Museum like quality, a glimpse to previous time.
Living history display from biblical times of Jacob and David,
Lone shepherd, lone dog, flock of sheep.
Simple.
Beauty.
Stillness,
Peace,
Safe.

Invisible Man

Invisible man,
Not what planned.
Present and not seen.
What can it mean?

Words spoken and not heard,
Musak™ like chirp of bird.
Ignored in bustle of life,
Supposedly soothes inner strife.

Not a magician's rabbit,
Shoved in a hat that doesn't fit.
Flee from that place,
So much life to embrace.

Come to Him

Always waiting for Him to come to me,
What would it be if reversed the role?
Me pursuing Him and being free,
Finding new love within my soul?

Expressions and memories created,
Marks made, tattoos dated.
Etched with love deep within,
Eternity's taste now begins.

Don't have to wait till pass away,
Lover's dance starts today.
Paradigm of intimacy shifts,
Oh, life what a gift.

Flaming Turkey or Ode to Differential Relays

When day doesn't go as planned,
Interrupted and kicked the can.
Turkey committed suicide,
Interrupting electricity in death's glide.

Erupted in fire,
Dead before hit the ground.
Poor turkey in different fryer,
Relays worked so carcass found.

One big bird disrupts so many,
Lights don't turn on.
Inspect the equipment,
Test the substation.

In memory to differential relays,
A carcass remains.
Anything else just a pile of goo,
That would remain unclaimed.

Heart Broker

Given my heart away,
Soul wandered and strayed.
Subtle at first,
Now unquenchable thirst.

Heart is lost,
I've paid horrible cost.
Came to my senses,
Yet soul tense.

There is One who can redeem,
The cost He paid was extreme.
He isn't afraid to rescue me,
He longs for me to be free.

Coyotes

Like ghosts the pair of coyotes moved silently down the property line,
In the predawn hour, double take as they lope weary this time.
They don't turn but know we are here,
They outrun all their fear.

Pinkish horizon painted on rippling clouds,
Just Molly and me, the silence loud.
Our early morning routine, peace as sun rises,
Grateful for another day with all its surprises.

In the distance hear the horses at the shed,
Restless and wanting to be fed.
They all face our way as return,
Bobbing heads, tummies yearn.

Faith Is

Faith is:

> The farmer working the ground.
> The farmer planting the seed.
> Risking again.
> Trying again.
> Letting go.
> Trusting.
> Believing.
> Hoping when nothing visible.
> Believing God is good.
> Repenting and believing forgiven.
> Courage to say I'm sorry.
> Hope of restoration.
> Hope of reconciliation.
> Knowing all will be made right in time.
> Not killing desires in disappointments.
> Honestly looking at the mess.
> Courage to truly see.

Highway 85 North of Cheyenne

Roads icy,
Blowing snow.
Drive so slow,
Gets dicey.

Visibility fades,
In light of day.
Ghostly white,
Snow dances light.

Fortitude

Another day begins,
Will I explore my soul within?
Easily get busy,
Heart becomes dizzy.

Fortitude required,
To not get stuck in quagmire.
Courage to say no,
Rest in love's glow.

Treasure buried deep,
In undiscovered soul's keep.
Locked behind vault's impenetrable door,
Combination to unlock found when explore.

Explore the hidden places,
Discover own motive of why.
Soul longs to come alive,
Spirit man yearning to thrive.

Chipping away at hardened heart,
Hear the chisel ring when hammer's strike starts.
Protective encasement releases,
All coping and numbness ceases.

Love makes supple and new,
When give up and thought through.
Seed that fell in the ground,
In due season it grew.

Pivot

Plant one foot and turn,
Allow love's tug and yearn.
Gaze shifts, transitions to another,
Explore intimacy undiscovered.

Depth of love a person can't fill,
Don't have to wait until...
Adventures with Him full of grace,
Press close to see His face.

This life will fade what's left?
Only what's forged with Him.
Change while still have breath,
Don't have to live bereft.

Love wins the day,
Conquers fear.
His presence near,
Even on days unclear.

Experienced love causes faith to grow,
Our hope in Him a fiery glow.
Warmth of His presence in darkest place,
With open arms I embrace.

Softly know He's come,
Hear His quiet hum.
Smile lightens face,
Endurance in life's race.

Ebbings

Sky gray,
Somber day.
Thoughts far away,
Often pray.

Struggle for life,
Death's slicing knife.
Strands slowly cut,
Anxiety in gut.

Life ebbing with each breath,
All just stare at death.
Examine heart,
Eternity stark.

Eternal brings perspective,
Deceived, finally seeing.
Eternity begins today,
No further delay.

Grief in letting them go,
Time slows.
Memories awaken,
Loved one can't truly be taken.

What Does Heart Say

What does heart say?
Mind constantly reasoning, not allowing heart to play.
Bully self with past scripts.
Scripts that etch into soul, not all are gifts.

Work to be done, not very fun.
What scripts lift up?
What scripts pull down?
Place of reality and raw awareness.

No longer a child.
Scripts aren't sacred.
Some scripts hinder intimacy.
It is time to lay those scripts on the altar.

Bondage to lose.
Freedom to gain.
Grace available to use.
Don't waste the pain.

Suffering rivets and rattles.
No longer satisfied with prattle.
Wakens long lost desires.
Igniting dormant fires.

Quid Pro Quo

People depressed and hopeless,
Believing best days are gone, copeless.
Politicians hawking their wares,
Make it about them so no one cares.

Gloom and doom,
From media outlets boom.
Flatulence that fills the room,
Stench of death in tomb.

Create a crisis to blame,
To them just political game.
Better yet set my opponent on fire,
Character doesn't matter to a liar.

Leadership vacuum today,
Take action, more than just pray.
Corporations and unions quid pro quo,
Let them "eat cake" as they go.

Legacy

Will they know my legacy,
When my last breath breathed?
What will be left,
What legacy will I leave?

Each day that goes by,
Planting seed for those who proceed.
Will they know of my love,
Will they build upon what I have given?

A father's desire for children to surpass,
To get a head start, not build from scratch.
Sown in love, truth, and courage,
Vulnerable, real, raw, and free.

A father who pressed in courageously,
Going places previous generations couldn't.
Being an example of love and courage,
Imparting love, courage, truthfulness, and boldness.

Building upon those gone before,
Launch pad for children to lift off.
Graceful and loving,
Loved while living.

Old Red Tractor

In the predawn darkness ether snorts into the engine's nostrils,
Slow grind of starter as tractor belches.
Coldness resisting the desire to start,
Yet ether is a powerful drug for diesel.

Finally ignition catches and rumble starts,
Hydraulics whine as cold blood shoots through the system.
As move the whine decreases,
Lowering the blade to move snow.

Driveway covered in seven inches,
Giving way to the red tractor's 60 horses.
Pushing piles of snow out of the way,
Brisk air brushes face, no cab to numb winter.

Daily Grind

Deer move about in snow.
Herds around Monument, one wants across road.
Brake 'til truck moving slow.
My presence a goad.

Turns around.
Unusual just one.
Away she bounds.
People shunned.

Beauty centers thoughts.
Calms the mind.
Mental battles fought.
Release from daily grind.

Anxiety

So want to control,
Hard to let go.
Anxiety shaken,
Desire for control awakens.

Want to control the weather today,
Force it to cooperate and hold at bay.
Consumes energy and time,
Crazy to think it's normal and fine.

Anxiety,
Anxiety.
Settle my soul,
Anxiety takes toll.

Fire in the Hole

Whatever hole fell in – fire in the hole.
In deepest, darkest place just a flicker of light brings hope to soul.
May believe all alone, that's a lie.
God brings hope, hears my cry.

In shadows alone must face.
Fear comes in darkest place.
Broken moment, overcome terror and set free.
One glimpse of light, anxiety flees.

No need to wallow.
Wasted years hard to swallow.
One glance of Him, all made right.
God's mercy such safe delight.

Mud

Mud all around.
Snow melts, soaking the ground.
Once covered white, now found.
Size reduced of the mound.

Warm enough to thaw.
Horses no longer paw.
Need bales of straw.
Between seasons life's raw.

Press on with blog.
Mud and bog.
A few more lines.
I'll be fine.

Soft Sky

Light of morning softly caresses mountain peaks,
Snowy summits, mauve colored sky streaks.
Majesty and grandeur loom to the West,
Soul comes alive, calls forth the best.

Lost in the hustle of another work day,
Just obliviously on our way.
Can't see the beauty before our eyes,
Creates incongruence, never slow to ponder why?

One more moment, another breath,
Stop and engage or just daily death?
Soft sky offers to give,
Invitation to live.

Beholding

What you see is what you get?
Could be worry, could be fret?
Could be joy, could be peace?
What do I see, soul's crease?

Holds my attention, fixes my gaze.
I run through life's maze.
Fixated on where my focus is.
Blindly going about my 'biz.'

Intentional focus, effort of correction,
Realize where my eyes go sets direction.
Beauty I behold,
Effects whether hot or cold.

Pray

What to do with all that surrounds?
Some as goofy as clowns.
Internal happiness yet to be found.
Others just frown.

Rub shoulders and no one knows.
The struggles and battles grow.
Façade covers as skin tight clothes.
Leaving nothing exposed.

Shutting down in a shell.
Wanting a magic spell.
Only to discover there isn't an easy way.
Driven to knees, pray.

Weight and Wait

When told to wait, burden added,
Weight of wait, agitates.
Not told yes, not told no,
Indifference and ambivalence in don't know.

Try to control the weight,
Yet crushes, presses, and resists.
Wait builds muscles,
Patience, empathy, humility all grow.

Suffering under wait,
Wanting delivered from weight.
Being human,
In this life all wrestle with wait.

Transparency

Dynamic to live in reality.
Transparency, allows self to be seen.
Congruent - internal fidelity.
Truth batters, grit abrasively restores sheen.

Repeatedly allow self to be conned.
Permit another to abuse, swindle.
Intentions good, yet allured and fawned.
Keenness of mind lost, cognition dwindles.

Must wake up, forbid mental seduction.
Truth and wholeness requires new deductions.

Coyote Carcass

Coyote carcass on our dirt road.
Cold and lifeless yet pelt looks warm.
Just a few hours ago he strode.
In the ditch he "bought the farm."

Curiosity gets the better of me.
I just caught a glance.
Backup the car so I can see.
Stare for a moment, mesmerized trance.

One less in the pack.
Howl no longer hear.
One less set of tracks.
A howl no longer clear.

Danced

Danced like young love.
Danced like well-aged love.
Danced like no one was watching.
Danced to our song - *Annie's Song*.

Danced and changed the atmosphere.
Danced and shared moments with others.
Danced and felt foolish as flow with the rhythm.
Danced and was alive.

Maturity

Resistance, internal core incongruent.
Mismatch, out of sync causing personal soul, mind, body, emotional, spirit dissonance.
Wrestling with alignment and belief.

Words I say matter.
How I treat others matters.
Apologizing matters.
Taking responsibility for what I've said and done matters.

Maturity demonstrated by actions.
Cleaning up mess made matters – humbling.
Admitting and asking for help matters.
Being truthful matters.
Hard, internal work for change.
All takes time, no "magic wand" – facing Truth and work.
Reflected in mirror of others.
DARVO, perpetrator-victim cycles.
Requires more than just forgiveness.
Requires internal work, revisiting suffering and trauma hidden.
Suffering and trauma caused by people – God uses people to bring healing to those broken places.

Maturity chooses to include safe people in process.
Maturity requires dealing with my interpretations and offenses.
Maturity is healthy growth over time – no quick fixes.
Maturity is about how I respond internally – exposes pride, control, fear, shame, abusiveness.

Maturity is saying I apologize for hurting you in _____ ways.
Maturity is saying you didn't deserve the way I acted, behaved, or treated you – specific!
Maturity says this is what I am doing to not do this again – specific.
Maturity says to one I hurt, you are valuable and worth more than how I behaved and words _____(specific) I said.
Maturity, seeing the harm I caused in and to another AND BEING

different.
Maturity, asking how did I hurt you? – not making excuses or justifying behavior.
Maturity, a journey can't travel alone.

Google DARVO if interested on meaning of the term. Eye opening.... I double dog dare you.

Loose Cannon

Term "loose cannon" floating in my mind as wake.
A loose cannon on an old warship (sailing ship) could wreck it.
A cannon broke loose, always when in rough seas wreaking havoc.
Hurting or killing the very ones who use it, hindering the ships created purpose.

At times we can be "loose cannons."
Abusive people are "loose cannons."
I can be a "loose cannon" – to myself and others.
Loose cannon in soul, damages and destroys self and relationships with others.

Words, anger, fear, shame, broke free in storms of life – "loose cannons."
People run for their lives away from "loose cannons."
A courageous few must anchor the "loose cannon" back to the deck.
Nimble, wise, seasoned, skilled, patient, disciplined shipmates secure the "loose cannon" and make the ship safe.
"Loose cannon" safe and secure.
Crew safe and secure.
Ship safe and secure.

Dreams

When a "bucket list" dream is near,
Years of wrestling and working becomes clear.
Put out there, exposed,
All that's decomposed.

Fertile soil in the until,
On the verge of harvest thrill.
To hold in hand,
On shore of new land.

Letting Go

Relationships transitioning,
New placement and positioning.
Rearrange what once has been,
Old places revisited and newly seen.

Cycles of life,
Birth and death soul pierced with knife.
Many births and deaths in each season,
Elements beyond control, beyond reason.

Grief waxes and wanes,
Ending and beginnings somber cool rain.
Wanting to know why,
When just need to cry.

Something New

Explore, try something new, path is unclear.
Overcome fear, anxieties disappear.
As play through the fear.
A new story to hear.

How often change story.
Lose Human glory.
To create reason to not try.
Exposes internal lies.
Stretch and grow.
Mind begins to glow.
Outcome stretches the mind.
New place to be kind.

Different format and venue.
Tasting new pallet foreign items on menu.
Some tastes delightful, other is bland.
Soul travels to new land.

Endurance

Word "Endurance" is indelibly married to Shackleton.
Overcoming all odds, persistent.
A place where training and discipline fill the space.

Endurance a place when hope falters and faith waivers.
Attitudes and beliefs become default.
Outcomes twisted, unclear, and lost – yet continue on.
"Trial by fire," smell of smoke, feel the heat.

Pressure building and building.
Moments when break, meltdown – transformed and remade.
Dying ember on ash heap sparks internal flame.
This won't be how my story ends.

No longer about circumstances and external visibility.
Body may be broken, yet a fighter is born.
Love does win.
In time or eternity will be made right, no more tears.

Dog Days

Dogs see me coming.
They are bored.
Making their day.
They've been anxiously waiting.

Led by the Border Collie.
Chow-Husky mix and a German Shepherd follow.
Race out to the road.
Brush the tires, dashing in front.

Waiting for me to gun the Explorer.
I wait 'til they tire.
Then make my break.
Forlorn they turn back to the house.

Boring dog day resumes.
Wishing for kids to play with.
Or a job to do.

Small Things

Small things add up over time.
Unseen things, that lead to "instant" success.
Struggles no one else knows.
Battles in the soul, leave a mark.

Only way forward is in the small daily struggle.
Five minutes here, fifteen there.
Invisible moments where faith and discipline meet.
Hope that as plant seed and discipline of daily tending will bear future harvest.

Silence in the discipline and internal growth.
Lonely place to be explored.
Fear exposed in risking.
Steps of faith.

Ice

Sun is bright yet ground is frozen.
Wind dances the powdery snow across the path.
Persistent and consistent glazing, donut like.
Drift builds up creeping its way across the path.

Surprised by the first patch of ice.
Grasp for traction.
Plod through small drifts.
Gingerly finding footing.

As day goes on more ice.
Scoop snow and ice still grows.
Sow gravel and sand on path.
Just another winter's day.

Cold Wind

Cold wind caresses face.
Body leans, propped and braced.
Cheeks redden as cool burns.
Direction headed reluctant to turn.

Bite of air, trudge along.
Chill requires motivation strong.
Each inhaled breath creates an ache.
Each exhaled breath leaves a foggy wake.

Eyes water in the breeze.
Squinting narrows vision, tears freeze.
Alive and aware in raw place.
No longer numb from routine, welcome grace.

Sunday Morning

Quiet Sunday morning.
Brilliant sunrise, day adorning.
Family still in bed.
Moments when soul is fed.

Bustle and rush soon begins.
Life awakens and blessed again.
Gifted another day to love.
Joy arises, birthed from above.

Out in the fields or in warmth of our home.
His goodness to us planted in soul's nurturing loam.
Hope in the new day, opportunities afresh.
Relationships and family engage and mesh.

Just the realization today of how long we've actually lived in Nebraska. How time sneaks up and before we know it another decade has past. So here's to "The Good Life."

28 Years

Away from completing college.
Living in Western Nebraska.
More time here than anyplace else.
Time ever advancing, sneakily.

Career, marriage, and family.
Transitions over time.
From city to country.
Friendships ebb and flow.

Time, life, and energy invested in one place.
Hopes, dreams, and what yet will be.
Past and present woven together with threads of life.
Just as family woven together in living life together.

Space Between Desires and Expectations

Expectations are fantasy outcomes in the mind.
Expectations may be based in familiar and deep wound want healed.
Desires are hopes and longings residing in soul.
Desires are places in soul needing expression.

Expectations project my "garbage" on another.
Expectations are false places based on what believe entitled to.
Desire releases need to control, freedom.
Desire dwells in journey of present moment.

Tension in space between desire and expectation.
Expectations hijack hopes, longings, and desires.
"Manage" expectations is just managing disappoint.
Healthy to live in place of satisfying relationship with desires, hopes, and longings.

Crack the Shell – Core Exposed

Those places sealed from moment of creation.
Cut open and exposed.
In darkness for decades.
Now cracked open to the light.

Covered in coldness, steel.
Protective casing cut.
Insulation exposed.
Dielectric covering no more.

Paper insulation once filled with oil.
Dripping free of impregnated insulating oil.
Moisture, once an enemy.
Now allowed to breathe free.

Gallons and gallons of oil.
Oil, light and highly refined removed.
Oil, copper, and steel to the recycler.
Melted down, repurposed, nothing wasted.

Molly - 1/2 Border Collie and 1/2 Pyrenees

Energy and motion.
Thrives in bitter cold.
Protect or herd?
Confused by instincts, loyal.

Big galute.
Loves me and is cute.
Happy to see me.
She knows a walk is coming.

Running free for ten minutes.
In her element, happy.
Joy to watch her,
Just be a dog.

Silence

Paradox of silence.
Tension of silence.
Moments when silence rejuvenates.
Moments when silence causes pain.

Silence can be maddening.
Silence can be electrifying.
Silence can feed anxiety and fear.
Silence can quiet soul.

Silence can fuel racing thoughts.
Silence can anchor soul to bedrock.
Silence can exasperate loneliness.
Silence can comfort in moments alone.

Broken Words - One for All and All for One

When words break,
Relationships change.
What once bound together,
Now cut free.

From long ago,
Words still echo.
Knocking down what tries to stand,
Yet damage done.

Forgiveness comes,
Time doesn't heal.
Pain still there,
Scars revealed.

Hope arises,
New circumstances.
Brings restoration,
Refreshing soul.

Internal change,
Navigate new way.
Letting "it" go,
Ever so slow.

Part I played,
How far we've strayed.
Hard roads walked,
Lessons still learning.

Don't waste the pain,
Allow God to use for gain.
Vulnerable and open,
Where restoration begins.

Veiled

Hidden and veiled.
Barrier between.
Image distorted.
Intimacy aborted.

Raise the veil.
Face to face.
Invasion of space.
Disruption of self in this place.

Look deep in the eyes.
Unhinged by the depths.
Relationship transformed.
In the lifting of the veil.

Fragile

Life is fragile.
Some things are fragile.
Usually they are important.
Perhaps priceless.

Often think of heirlooms, artwork, precious metals, or gems.
Overlooked are those I love the most.
I don't treat them as valuable, perhaps out of familiarity?
I don't steward them as they deserve - as priceless.

When those I love are broken or hurting,
Have I let them know their worth to me?
Perhaps I have been the one who chipped their fragile pieces.
Own it, "clean up the mess", let them know, be different… change!

Raw

Raw like hunk of meat.
Soul exposed on meat hook.
Exposed in open air, life unraveled.
Flavor added in cure time.

Hide ripped off.
Guts spilled out.
Carcass all that remains.
Carved up.

Moments in life when soul raw.
Vulnerable and exposed.
Press through fear pushing to "cut and run."
Allowing time to "cure," for healing.

Interpretations and meanings.
Wrestling with past and present.
Truth wages war with shame and fear.
Will I choose love; or shame and fear?

What will I believe?
What will I hope for?
Will I allow faith to rise up?
Will I dare to allow God's interpretation and meaning?

Healing does come.
Usually not in way expected.
Not in time expected.
Part of journey.

God is faithful.
He is good.
In the midst of suffering.
He comes, He sees, He comforts.

Notes

Notes

ABOUT THE AUTHOR

Brian and his wife, along with their three children, reside on the western edge of Nebraska. From their small farm they have a distant view of Laramie Peak in Wyoming. They have lived in Western Nebraska for the past 28 years.

Among Brian's eclectic interests are Border Collies, Australian Shepherds and herding dogs; photography; writing; and teaching. He has a degree in mechanical engineering.

You can see more of Brian's writings at http://www.westernnebraskathoughtsandlife.com (blog) and at http://www.westernnebraskapoet.com (website).

www.ingramcontent.com/pod-product-compliance
Lightning Source LLC
Chambersburg PA
CBHW071739040426
42446CB00012B/2401